Charlotte's Web

The Essential Guide

Charlotte's Web

The Essential Guide

Written by Amanda Li

4

Contents

Salutations, readers!

It's dark up in this corner and you might not be able to see us – after all, we're only little spiders. Well, anyway, we'd like to introduce ourselves to you. We're Charlotte's daughters and we're staying in this big old barn – it's where our mother once lived, you know! We were born here a month ago and the three of us have been having a ball ever since. We've got this great web going at the top of the doorway where you can see all the animals that live below. There's a horse, some geese, lots of sheep and two really funny cows. They make us laugh a lot!

Our best friend of all is Wilbur. He's a pig and he thinks our mother would have been proud of us. He says that she was a brilliant and beautiful spider who was the most loyal friend anyone could ever have. You might wonder how a pig and a spider could become such great friends. Here is their story.

Joy, Aranea
and Nellie

Fern

Twelve-year-old Fern Arable is a girl of action. Strong-willed, spirited and stubborn, she saves a young pig's life by standing up to her father. She's a true animal lover. And being raised on a farm means Fern has plenty of time to spend with her animal friends.

Good strong arms for fighting

Tattered dungarees

Fearless

Tearing around the farmyard, swinging up high on the barn rope, scrapping with her brother – it's fair to say that Fern is a regular tomboy.

Pig in peril

When a new litter of piglets is born, Fern is outraged to find her father about to kill the tiny runt. As a farmer, he believes it's the kindest thing to do.

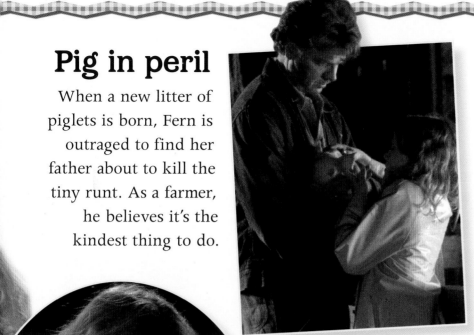

Unusual pupil

Fern misses the farm while she's at school, so she brings a little reminder with her. But keeping a lid on it isn't as easy as she thought!

Fern's desk contains pens, pencils – and a hungry piglet!

Lifesaver

'If I'd been small, would you have killed me?' Fern demands. Mr Arable gives in and lets her keep the piglet. She calls her new pet Wilbur.

Animal talk

- Fern has a natural affinity with animals. She understands them and they understand her.
- Fern doesn't have many human friends – her best friends are her *beast* friends!
- Most people, Fern's mother in particular, don't believe that Fern can have real conversations with animals.

Fern listens closely to her new friend Wilbur.

Wilbur

Meet Wilbur. Like most young pigs, he's very cute. But there's much more to Wilbur than a dinky little snout and long fluttering eyelashes. He's a pig with a personality. Loyal, friendly, honest and sincere, Wilbur possesses some wonderful qualities. In fact, he's probably the nicest, most good-hearted creature you're ever likely to meet.

A poorly piglet

One of a litter of nine piglets, poor little Wilbur was the runt: small, sickly and unlikely to survive. That is, until Fern came along.

Appealing long-lashed eyes

The smallest pig of the litter.

Pampered pig

Wilbur may have lost his birth mother, but he quickly gains another mother in the shape of Fern. She adores Wilbur and loves looking after him.

Sensitive snout can sniff out slops

Pig facts

- Many people believe that pigs are dirty animals but this is not true. Pigs can't sweat so they need to roll in mud or water to keep cool.
- A female pig is called a sow. Sows usually give birth to eight to twelve babies (a litter) at a time.
- Pigs are intelligent, sensitive creatures who have a natural sense of curiosity. They are thought to be more intelligent than dogs.

Favourite things

One of Wilbur's favourite things is glorious, squelchy mud. He loves rolling in it, splashing in it, wriggling in it and sliding through it. His all-time favourite food is slops – leftovers such as potato peelings, apple cores and bread crusts. But most of all, Wilbur loves spending time with his favourite person, Fern.

Like most pigs, Wilbur is extemely sensitive and he hates being alone.

Porcine pal

Wilbur is a sociable creature – he likes company, adores conversation and loves making friends. Fern becomes his first real pal but he soon makes lots of others when he arrives at the Zuckermans' barn.

The Arables

Fern's parents, Mr and Mrs Arable, are both practical, down-to-earth people who are busy running a farm, a house and raising two energetic children. Managing the farm means that Mr Arable is usually found driving a tractor or ploughing the fields. Caring and affectionate Mrs Arable makes sure that the children are fed, dressed and on time for school. But the one thing she hasn't succeeded in is making Fern wear a dress!

Tousled hair is hard to control – just like Avery!

Mr Arable

Like most farmers, Mr Arable believes that pigs make great bacon, not great pets. But he respects Fern's protectiveness towards animals.

The Farm

Wilbur doesn't need to travel far to his new home. The Arables and the Zuckermans are neighbours and their farms are close to each other, separated only by a winding country road.

Arable barn

This is where Wilbur was born and where he has spent most of his life so far.

Arable house

This cosy farmhouse is the centre of family life for Fern, Avery and Mr and Mrs Arable.

The dump

Fortunately, the smelly rubbish dump is located well away from both farms. Only scavengers such as crows and rats enjoy sniffing around in the stinking mess.

The Zuckermans

Fern's uncle and aunt, Homer and Edith Zuckerman, are close relatives of the Arables; so close, in fact, that they live right next door. The Zuckermans even follow the family tradition of running a farm. And, as Mrs Arable suggests, they're the ideal couple to take in Wilbur when he grows too big for the Arables' place.

Homer considers giving Wilbur a home

Homer Zuckerman

Homer works hard from dusk till dawn, along with his trusty farm animals. At the end of the day, the animals go back to the barn while Homer puts his feet up back at the farmhouse.

Here comes trouble!

Ten-year-old Avery Arable is Fern's annoying little brother. He wreaks havoc with his wooden sword and even tries to capture a spider using a pitchfork! Perhaps his most memorable misdemeanour is when he accidentally steps on a rotten egg in the barn and creates an enormous stink. Eeeew!

Where Avery goes, mayhem usually follows.

Calm expression conceals deeper concerns

Perplexed parent

Mrs Arable worries about her daughter spending so much time with a pig. When Fern lets it slip that she talks to animals, Mrs Arable visits Doctor Dorian. He believes Fern suffers from a common condition called "childhood". Mrs Arable isn't so sure. Maybe it's time for Wilbur to go.

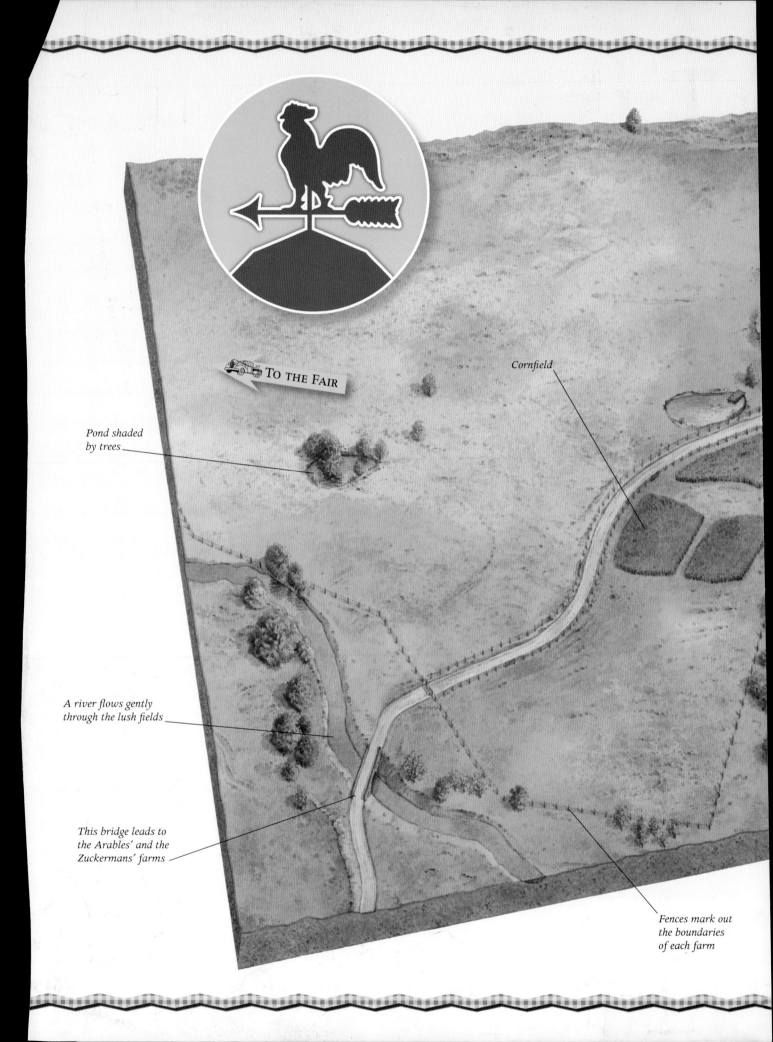

TO THE FAIR

Cornfield

Pond shaded
by trees

A river flows gently
through the lush fields

This bridge leads to
the Arables' and the
Zuckermans' farms

Fences mark out
the boundaries
of each farm

Tasty treats

The Zuckermans grow lots of fruit and vegetables. Edith is well known for her homemade jams – made from fruits grown in her own garden.

Freshly-picked apples from the orchard

Look out, Lurvy!

Lurvy is the Zuckermans' accident-prone farmhand. When he tries to catch Wilbur, Lurvy gets tangled up in a scarecrow and falls, flattening a row of beans. Deep in conversation with a pretty lady, he casually leans against an unlocked gate. It opens up and he tumbles to the ground. Whoops!

A new addition

Homer and Edith decide what to do about Wilbur. Is there room in their barn for one little piglet? The answer is yes! And Wilbur arrives soon afterwards.

Zuckerman barn

Wilbur's first impression of the barn is that it's big! And it needs to be – it's home to a flock of sheep, some cows, geese and even a horse. Will they welcome a pig?

Smokehouse

Few animals can bear to mention the scary smokehouse. Out of sight, at the back of the farm, it's the place where pigs go in – and bacon comes out.

Zuckerman house

This large attractive farmhouse is where Homer and Edith Zuckerman live. The most important room is the kitchen, where Edith does all her baking and jam-making.

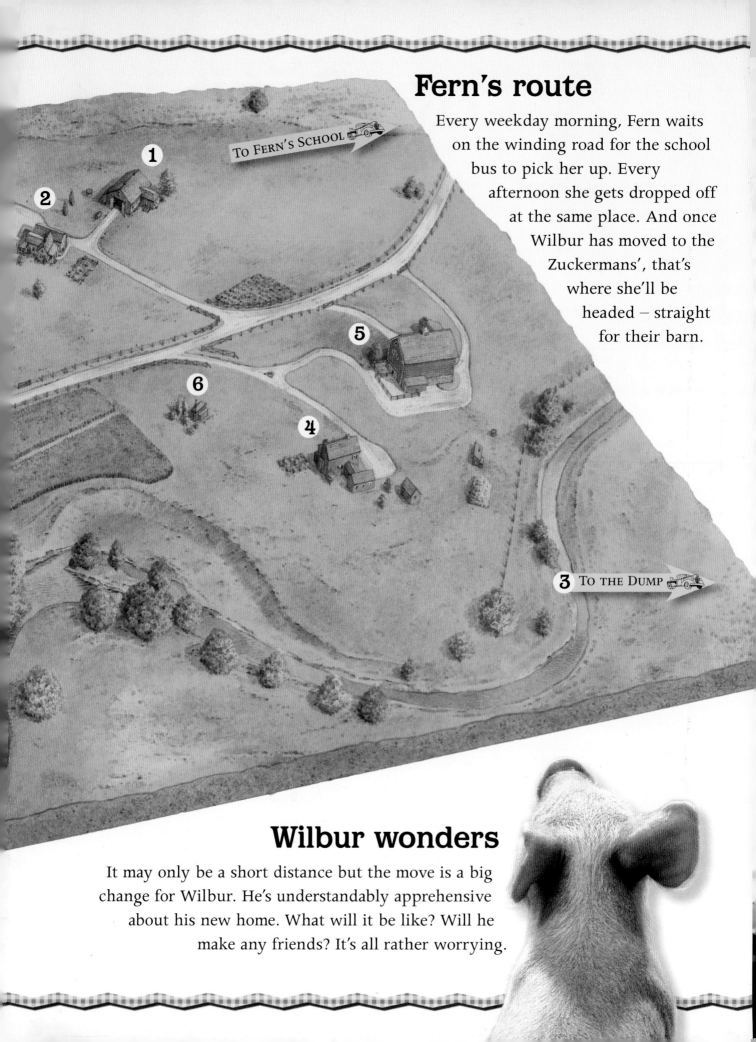

Fern's route

Every weekday morning, Fern waits on the winding road for the school bus to pick her up. Every afternoon she gets dropped off at the same place. And once Wilbur has moved to the Zuckermans', that's where she'll be headed – straight for their barn.

TO FERN'S SCHOOL

3 TO THE DUMP

Wilbur wonders

It may only be a short distance but the move is a big change for Wilbur. He's understandably apprehensive about his new home. What will it be like? Will he make any friends? It's all rather worrying.

The Barn

An apprehensive Fern takes Wilbur to his new home. It's a huge, weathered old farm building with high ceilings, wooden rafters and hay-strewn floors. When sunlight streams in through the windows, it's almost beautiful. But Wilbur can only think of Fern and how much he's going to miss her when she leaves.

Homely aroma

The barn has a very distinctive smell. Two parts horse sweat, one part old rope, a portion of cow dung, some feathers and an old work boot – all topped off with a splash of diesel fuel.

Wilbur puts on a brave face to greet his new companions.

Boring beasts

The barn's residents are a flock of sheep, a pair of geese, two cows, a horse and a rat. Wilbur tries to persuade them to play with him but they're not interested. That night, he goes to bed a lonely pig.

Fern is always delighted to see her best friend

New-look barn

- The shabby barn is later transformed into a handsome building.
- Homer paints the walls a beautiful shade of burnt red. The windows and fence get a fresh coat of paint too.
- Visitors are now greeted by an impressive-looking dwelling – and the animals have a lovely home.

Friends forever

Wilbur thought he would never see Fern again but he needn't have worried. Fern comes to the barn to visit Wilbur every day, rain or shine, school day or weekend. They may live apart but they're still the closest of friends.

Wilbur's new home gets a fresh new look.

Charlotte

The first new friend that Wilbur makes is a spider. But Charlotte A. Cavatica is no ordinary spider. Clever, charming and creative, she spins incredible webs – which sparks off her brilliant idea to help Wilbur. But despite her talents, most creatures react with a disgusted 'Yeuuch!' when they first see her. To Wilbur, however, she is simply beautiful.

A fateful meeting

Wilbur first talks to Charlotte in the dark. He has no idea that he's talking to a spider. The next day, when he finally sees the owner of the soft voice, he's surprised – then horrified – to see her sinking her fangs into a struggling fly. But Wilbur soon gets over it and the pair become the best of friends.

A promise to a pig

When Avery tries to capture Charlotte in a jar, Wilbur saves her. So when Wilbur makes the terrible discovery that he won't live to see Christmas, Charlotte vows to save his life in return. But how? Charlotte reassures him: 'I don't know but I will not let them kill you.'

Long scuttling legs enable quick movement

Sophisticated, clever mind

Scary, hairy appearance terrifies some creatures

Sophisticated spider

Charlotte appreciates the beauty of language. She's very particular about finding the right word for the job and likes to use highly descriptive phrases, some of which cause bewilderment among the farm animals. Sometimes Charlotte needs to explain her cultured quotations!

Quotations

- *Salutations* – as Charlotte says, "This is just a fancy way of saying 'Hello'".
- *Sotto voce* – when Charlotte asks Wilbur to sing like this, she's saying sing "to yourself".
- *Magnum Opus* – means "great work". And Charlotte is quietly working away on her own magnum opus, one that will be revealed in time.

Gussy and Golly

Gussy and Golly are the old married couple of the barn. Gussy is a bossy wife who quite literally rules the roost, bringing new meaning to the phrase 'henpecked' – or should that be 'goosepecked'? Poor old Golly always seems to be putting his foot in it, which is when Gussy lets him have it with a good hard thrash of her wing. Ouch!

Strong wings keep Gussy's husband in place

A day to remember

Gussy's short temper might be because she's nesting, sitting on her precious eggs to keep them safe and warm. When the big hatching day comes, seven little goslings emerge from the eggs. With their soft downy heads and tiny beaks they're just the sweetest things the farm animals have ever seen!

Goose facts

- All geese can inflict painful blows with their wings if provoked.

- Some types of geese pair up for life. The male goose (called the gander) helps to protect and raise the young.

- The female usually lays four to seven eggs, which take three or four weeks to hatch. The young goslings stay with their parents for the first year of life.

Gussy gets into a flap!

Betsy and Bitsy

The double act of the barn, Betsy and Bitsy are two cows who really know how to enjoy themselves. They find most things "a-moo-sing", particularly the other farm animals, who end up on the receiving end of their many jokes. Not only do the bovine best friends share a sense of humour, they also have the same easygoing, relaxed attitude to life.

Rumble in the farmyard

If Betsy and Bitsy are around, you're sure to know about it. This pair of parping pals break wind at any opportunity, creating a most unpleasant atmosphere in the barn. Neither creature is embarrassed in the slightest by their windy ways. They'll happily let rip until the cows come home.

Wilbur gazes at his new home, unaware of the rumbling noise in the corner

Bitsy delivers one of her punchlines

Pull the udder one

Like a couple of giggling schoolgirls, you'll always find the ladies chuckling about something. When Wilbur escapes from his pen, there's a cry of "Pig's out!" Bitsy responds, "He sure is – out of his mind!"

Flatulent cow facts

There's no doubt that Betsy and Bitsy are a couple of windbags. Here's why:

- Cows have four-chambered stomachs, designed for breaking down large quantities of grass and plant matter.

- They eat fast, storing their food in the first stomach chamber. Billions of bacteria and organisms live here and turn the plant matter into methane gas. The gas is released by breaking wind or belching.

Contented – but full of gas.

Ike and Samuel

Ike is a horse. Samuel is a sheep. The two creatures do have something in common though – both the haughty horse and the snobbish sheep like nothing better than the sound of their own voices. Samuel has always got something to say on barn affairs while Ike is well-known for telling very long, very boring stories about his great grandfather. Yawn…

Always watching over his flock

Never lost for words

Leader of the flock

Samuel has an entire flock of sheep hanging on his every word. If he likes something, they like it. If he changes his mind, they follow suit. As Gussy says, "Not one brain between them!"

Ears focus on his own voice

Personal remarks

The residents of the barn aren't exactly polite about each other. In fact, Ike is downright rude about Samuel's woolly coat when he says "I shudder to think of what's crawling around inside it".

orrifed horse

looks big and strong but he's terrified
spiders. When he first sees Charlotte, he
nics, kicks at his door and shouts "GET IT
VAY!" When she sinks her fangs into a
uggling fly, it's all too much. Ike faints.

Ike rears up in fear.

*Enjoys listening
to himself*

*Proud self-
important
expression*

Scary spiders

- A lot of people have a fear of spiders.
  In extreme cases this is called arachnophobia.

- Arachnophobes may break out in a sweat,
  feel sick, have trouble breathing or even
  faint if they see a spider.

- No one is quite sure why spiders cause such
  extreme reactions but it might be because
  of their scuttling movement.

Templeton

He's greedy, he's sharp-tongued and he's unbelievably selfish. Meet Templeton, the barn's resident rat. Templeton is a born survivor, scavenging for scraps of food and living by his wits. To him, life is simple. There are just two things to think about – Templeton, closely followed by Templeton's stomach.

Monster appetite

This ravenous rodent can eat like a horse and will devour practically anything until he reaches bursting point. Luckily for Templeton the entrance to his lair is directly next to Wilbur's brimming trough.

Mr Unpopular

Helping others? Nope, that's not Templeton's thing. Not unless he gets something worthwhile out of it himself. He eventually agrees to help Wilbur but only because he doesn't want to see his supply of slops disappear.

Ratty remarks

The smart-talking rat is never lost for words.

- On being a rat of simple means: "I gnaw. I spy. I eat. I hide. Me in a nutshell."

- On being called "just a rat": "For your information, pig, the RAT rules".

- On being splattered with rotten egg: "Guess the yolk's on me. Heh, heh."

Templeton rolls the rotten egg away from Gussy and Golly's nest.

Tactless

Templeton is the only barn animal brutal enough to tell Wilbur the terrible truth – that once winter arrives, pigs end up as sausages and ham. Wilbur can't believe his ears. Surely humans love pigs? The rat is quick to point out that they love pork just as much.

Beady eyes search for interesting finds

A snout that can sniff out a snack in a second

The Lair

Only Templeton knows that the dark hole next to Wilbur's trough is the doorway to a secret world. When the rat darts into this tunnel he makes his way through a winding network of passageways to reach a special place – his underground lair. The place is full to the brim with all kinds of junk but to Templeton it's a glittering treasure trove. He's spent years collecting his precious things.

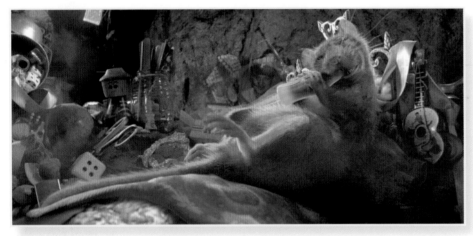

Relaxed rat

Templeton has worked hard to make his den just the way he likes it. As he lies back on his comfy bed with a delicious cola bottle he sighs with pleasure: "Aaah - it's good to be me!"

Lair Key

1 A shiny key makes an attractive ceiling decoration

2 Playing cards decorate the wall

3 Templeton's treasured bottle collection

4 This stick wasn't easy to bring in – but Templeton managed it!

5 A second tunnel leads out of the lair

6 Cosy chair is a tuna can stuffed with sheep's wool

7 Refreshments are always available

8 An old bit of fabric is used as a bedspread

9 Cardboard makes great table tops

Charlotte's Webs

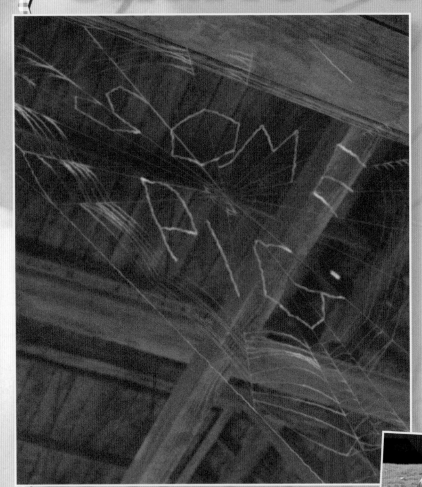

Charlotte promised Wilbur that she wouldn't let him be killed. But she must move fast to save her friend's life. While Wilbur sleeps, Charlotte thinks hard as she rebuilds her web. Suddenly, she stops. The dangling threads are making a shape – a faint letter "S". Inspiration strikes In the morning, an incredible sight awaits the farm's inhabitants There, glistening in the light, are two beautifully spun words: "SOME PIG".

A word spun by a spider? Homer and Lurvy do a double take.

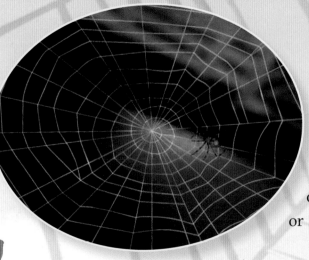

Wonderful webs

There are several different types of web. The kind that Charlotte spins is called the orb web and it is usually found among plants or in corners of buildings or fences.

Spider facts

- Spiders are very useful to humans because they feed on insects such as flies and mosquitos.

- Ever wondered why spiders don't get caught in their own webs? The clever creatures stay free by coating their legs with a special oily substance secreted from their mouths.

- Spiders webs are easily damaged, so they spend a lot of time repairing and rebuilding them.

Charlotte can repair her web in seconds.

In a spin

Like all spiders, Charlotte has three pairs of glands at the back of her body called spinnerets. These produce thin jets of liquid silk that quickly harden in the air as she spins, making strong and sticky threads.

Delicate but deadly

With their shimmering strands and pretty patterns, Charlotte's webs are truly beautiful. But to an insect, a web is a death trap. Once a struggling bug gets caught up in those sticky strands, its fate is sealed. Charlotte will paralyse it with a poisonous bite — then the feast begins.

The Famous Farm

The Zuckermans' farm is usually a quiet and peaceful place. But when news spreads about the miraculous web, it's a heaving mass of excited people. Homer realises this is a great business opportunity and soon the Zuckermans are selling homemade lemonade, apples and other farm goods to an appreciative audience. What a day!

Brisk business

Within moments, Edith has set up a 'drive-through' stall, loaded with fresh farm fruits. And there are plenty of customers just ripe for the picking.

Edith's famous and delicious Applesauce is one of her best-sellers.

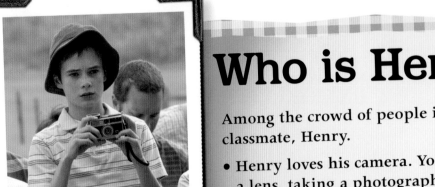

Henry and his prized possessions.

Who is Henry Fussy?

Among the crowd of people is a familiar face – Fern's classmate, Henry.

- Henry loves his camera. You'll always find him behind a lens, taking a photograph of something interesting.
- Henry likes to wear his green fishing hat most of the time.
- Fern catches sight of Henry on a fence, trying to get a shot of the web. They smile at each other for the first time.

Who's who

Nearly everyone seems to be at the Zuckermans' farm – close friends and neighbours, townsfolk who've heard the gossip, local photographers and journalists desperate to get a good story.

Wilbur's moment of fame is captured by the cameras.

Wilbur the star

So, what does Wilbur think of all this unexpected attention? He loves it! As he poses and smiles for the cameras, everyone can see that he really is "SOME PIG". And no one is prouder of him than Fern.

The Emergency Meeting

After the crowds have gone, the farm is quiet once again. But Charlotte is anxious. She knows that humans have short memories and the "miracle" of the web is already last week's news. To be certain of saving Wilbur's life, another web must quickly be spun. But what will it say? Charlotte calls all the barn animals together to help.

An unappreciative audience

Wilbur trusts Charlotte with his life – and she won't let him down.

The meeting doesn't get off to a good start. One of the cows breaks wind. Golly's laughter earns him a well-aimed whack from his wife. And Ike is still terrified of Charlotte so he stands facing away from her. Poor Charlotte!

Wise words

Charlotte explains to the animals that words are powerful things and must be chosen extremely carefully. What they decide to say about Wilbur could mean the difference between life and death. Her straight talking works – and the animals get thinking.

Web words

The creatures come up with a few rejects before hitting on the right description:

- "Harmoniously proportioned" – over-long and fussy

- "Pig Supreme" – sounds too much like a tasty dish!

- "Average" – just not exciting enough

- Gussy's idea – "terrific, terrific, terrific" – is much better. Take off two words and it's just about perfect!

A work of art

Watching Charlotte spin is an incredible sight; she drops her line, she falls and swings, attaching silky strands here and there as she zooms about. The animals gaze in wonder as the word "TERRIFIC" slowly but surely appears.

This web is truly terrific!

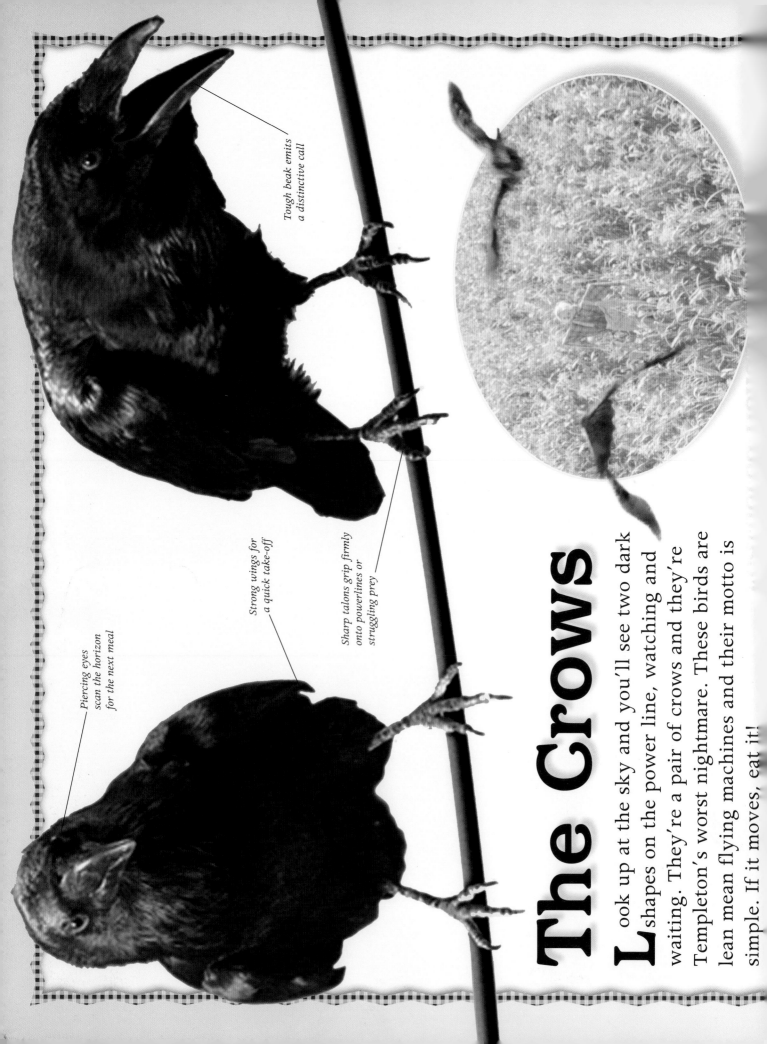

The Crows

Look up at the sky and you'll see two dark shapes on the power line, watching and waiting. They're a pair of crows and they're Templeton's worst nightmare. These birds are lean mean flying machines and their motto is simple. If it moves, eat it!

Tough beak emits a distinctive call

Sharp talons grip firmly onto powerlines or struggling prey

Strong wings for a quick take-off

Piercing eyes scan the horizon for the next meal

The crows hang out at the local rubbish dump, surveying the area in search of leftovers or, even better, live prey. As Templeton has learned only too well, if the crows spot a likely victim, they move fast. Templeton had a lucky escape when the crows became covered in pink paint, but a rat can never be too careful...

Fair game

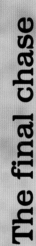

When Templeton visits the dump, he is horrified to find the beady-eyed birds waiting for him. They swoop down for a nasty peck. Templeton hides underneath a popcorn box, ready to make a run for it. He gets away – just.

The final chase

Charlotte has some excellent advice for the exhausted Templeton – lay a trap and wait patiently. The cunning rodent spots some netting draped over a shooting gallery and gets an idea. The next time the birds attack, he's ready. He lets them chase him up to the net, but leaps away at the last minute. Bam! Crows caught!

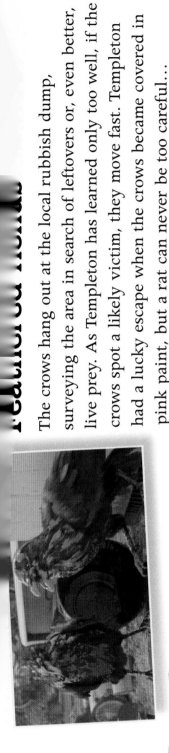

Crow facts

- Crows eat a huge variety of foods, including fruit, vegetables, insects, worms, frogs, snails and rodents.
- A group of crows is called a "murder".
- Crows communicate with each other by means of their loud, distinctive "Caawww!" Their cry sends messages such as warnings and fight signals.
- Crows are incredibly intelligent birds, with sharp eyesight and superb hearing.

Bold and aggressive? That pretty much sums up these two cunning crows.

A Radiant Pig

Charlotte believed that her words would save Wilbur – but a chance remark from Mr Zuckerman reveals that her friend is still in danger. She persuades Templeton to go in search of another word. The rat makes for the dump where, after a terrifying encounter with the crows, he discovers a scrap of magazine with the words "NEW RADIANT ACTION" printed on it. Time for a new web!

Fern's brainwave

When Fern realises the County Fair is coming up, she has a great idea – if Wilbur could win the pig competition, he'd be saved from the smokehouse. Clever Fern leaves the fair flier on Uncle Homer's desk.

Buttermilk bath

Who needs bubbles when you've got buttermilk?

- In preparation for the fair Mrs Zuckerman gives Wilbur the best clean-up of his life – a bath in rich buttermilk.

- Wilbur grunts with pleasure as she scrubs him all over with the cool, delicious liquid.

- Underneath him an equally delighted Templeton is lying on his back, slurping up the dripping buttermilk.

Judgement day

Homer decides to enter Wilbur in the competition. When it's time to leave for the big event, Charlotte travels along with Wilbur and Lurvy in the truck – and at the last moment Templeton is persuaded to jump in too.

Exciting news

Something strange is happening to Charlotte. She's getting heavier by the day and is feeling very tired indeed. She lets Wilbur into her secret – she's pregnant! Wilbur is delighted to hear her news.

The County Fair

Finally, the most talked-about event of the year arrives — the County Fair. Taking place over a week, the fair is a whirlwind of fun, food and farming events. All the townsfolk dress in their best, the Arables and the Zuckermans among them. Fern is incredibly excited — not only has Wilbur got an important competition to enter, she's got the run of the funfair and her own money to spend!

The Ferris wheel dominates the fairground with its incredible height and colourful lights.

Fern is having the time of her life!

Henry is on a high. Is it the Ferris wheel or Fern?

All the fun of the fair

The fair is full of the most wonderful stalls and rides but the most thrilling of all is the gigantic Ferris wheel. The sensation of soaring up, up into the sky and then swooping down is simply unforgettable. Fern and Henry are hooked and go on the ride again and again.

Prize pig

Every year the local farmers bring their best animals to the fair to compete for prizes. The Zuckermans hope that Wilbur will win the best pig award. Charlotte, Wilbur and Fern are hoping he'll win it too – because coming first means that Wilbur's life will be saved.

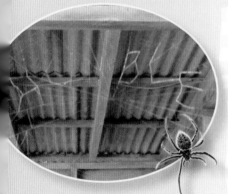

One last web

Charlotte knows the competition will be tough so she sends Templeton out in search of a new word for Wilbur. He finds one that is perfect – "HUMBLE"– and she spins it over Wilbur's pen.

Ravenous rat

- Templeton is lured to the fair by the promise of food. And he hasn't been let down.

- Everywhere he looks there are leftover scraps of hot dogs, popcorn, toffee apples and more. It's a rat's dream come true!

- By the time the fair ends, Templeton is nauseous, sticky and completely bloated – but he couldn't be happier.

Mmm... rat heaven!

The Judging Ring

Charlotte has spun her last web for the humble Wilbur. Now everything rests on the competition results. But before the prizes are officially announced Fern makes a shocking discovery. Another pig has won the prize! It's a dreadful moment. But minutes later a smiling fair official arrives to take Wilbur along to the judging ring.

When Fern hears that ano[th]er pig has won the competit[ion] she's inconsolable. Wha[t] will happen to Wilbur?

A very big pig

- The winning pig is in the pen next door to Wilbur. His name is Uncle.

- Uncle is absolutely enormous. Charlotte can hardly believe her eyes when she sees him for the first time.

- He's also a little slow — Uncle has trouble remembering his name and isn't sure of his age.

Everything is huge about Uncle, except for his brain.

There is loud applause as Fern proudly leads Wilbur around the ring.

The famous pig

Wilbur gets a wonderful surprise – a special award! Now he truly is a prize-winning pig.

Wilbur wears his medal and he couldn't be prouder!

Goodbye Charlotte

Wilbur's happiness fades when he hears devastating news. Charlotte's life is coming to an end and she won't be returning to the barn. It's time to say "Goodbye" – forever.

After Charlotte

Life after Charlotte just isn't the same. Everyone in the barn misses her wise words and warm personality. Wilbur feels it the most, after all, he has lost his dearest friend. But Charlotte has left something behind – her precious egg sac. Wilbur guards it carefully until all her 514 baby spiders have emerged! But only three decide to stay with Wilbur – Joy, Aranea and Nellie.

Aranea

Nellie

Joy

A pig at peace

Wilbur is contented and happy. He knows he will now live to see many more winters – all thanks to a very special spider. Charlotte may be gone, but her spirit lives on in her daughters.

Then and now

There have been a few changes in the barn since Charlotte's time. The good news is that Templeton has mellowed. The bad news is that he's so fat he can hardly walk! And incredibly, Ike is no longer terrified of spiders – he even makes friends with Joy, Aranea and Nellie.

A new Fern

Fern has changed, too. Now and then she'll be seen wearing a dress and a pretty ribbon in her hair. And she's not visiting the barn so much these days – she's spending a lot more time with Henry instead. Young Fern is growing up.

Grandfather Henry still wears a green hat!

Fern is now a grandmother but she will always remember her childhood friends

New generation

When many years have passed, Fern tells her granddaughter about a very special spider who saved a pig's life. Charlotte's webs will never be forgotten.

Fern and Henry's granddaughter is entranced by the story

DK

LONDON, NEW YORK, MUNICH,
MELBOURNE AND DELHI

EDITOR	*Amy Junor*
SENIOR DESIGNER	*Thelma-Jane Robb*
ASSISTANT DESIGNER	*Mika Kean-Hammerso*
SENIOR EDITOR	*Lindsay Kent*
PUBLISHING MANAGER	*Simon Beecroft*
BRAND MANAGER	*Robert Perry*
CATEGORY PUBLISHER	*Alex Allan*
DTP DESIGNER	*Hanna Ländin*
PRODUCTION	*Rochelle Talary*

First published in Great Britain in 2007 by
Dorling Kindersley Limited
80 Strand, London WC2R 0RL

07 08 09 10 10 9 8 7 6 5 4 3 2 1

A CIP catalogue for this book is available from the British Library.

ISBN: 978-1-40531-528-9

Colour reproduction by Media Development and Printing Ltd., UK

Printed and bound in China by Toppan.

ACKNOWLEDGEMENTS
The Publishers would like to thank Raina Moore and Laura Gilbert.

Discover more at
www.dk.com